Ecosystems
Caves

Erinn Banting

www.av2books.com

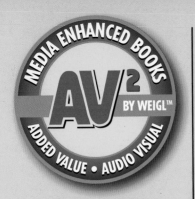

AV[2] provides enriched content that supplements and complements this book. Weigl's AV[2] books strive to create inspired learning and engage young minds in a total learning experience.

Your AV[2] Media Enhanced books come alive with...

Audio
Listen to sections of the book read aloud.

Key Words
Study vocabulary, and complete a matching word activity.

Video
Watch informative video clips.

Quizzes
Test your knowledge.

Embedded Weblinks
Gain additional information for research.

Slide Show
View images and captions, and prepare a presentation.

Try This!
Complete activities and hands-on experiments.

... and much, much more!

Go to **www.av2books.com,** and enter this book's unique code.

BOOK CODE

Z 4 5 4 6 7 7

AV[2] by Weigl brings you media enhanced books that support active learning.

Published by AV[2] by Weigl
350 5th Avenue, 59th Floor
New York, NY 10118
Website: www.av2books.com   www.weigl.com

Library of Congress Cataloging-in-Publication Data

Banting, Erinn.
 Caves / Erinn Banting.
    p. cm. -- (Ecosystems)
 Includes index.
 ISBN 978-1-61690-639-9 (hardcover : alk. paper) -- ISBN 978-1-61690-645-0 (softcover : alk. paper)
 1. Cave ecology--Juvenile literature. I. Title.
 QH541.5.C3B36 2011
 577.5'84--dc22
                          2010050985

Printed in the United States of America in North Mankato, Minnesota
1 2 3 4 5 6 7 8 9 0 15 14 13 12 11

052011
WEP37500

Project Coordinator Aaron Carr
Design Sonja Vogel

Every reasonable effort has been made to trace ownership and to obtain permission to reprint copyright material. The publishers would be pleased to have any errors or omissions brought to their attention so that they may be corrected in subsequent printings.

Photo Credits
Weigl acknowledges Getty Images as its primary photo supplier for this title.

Contents

What is a Cave Ecosystem?

The conelike rock formations found in many caves are formed over time by drops of water that leave mineral deposits behind.

Earth is home to millions of different **organisms**, all of which have specific survival needs. These organisms rely on their environment, or the place where they live, for their survival. All plants and animals have relationships with their environment. They interact with the environment itself, as well as the other plants and animals within the environment. These interactions create an **ecosystem**.

Each of Earth's seven continents is home to caves, from the frozen northern and southern poles to the tropical regions near the equator. They can be located under mountains, in the ocean, on islands, and even inside **glaciers**.

Caves are made up of small and large **caverns**, deep pits, underground waterways, and strange-looking rock formations. They provide a hiding place for natural wonders and animals seeking shelter.

Some animals, such as bears, use caves for warmth, shelter, and safety throughout their winter **hibernation**. Caves have also been used throughout history to hide and protect people, precious goods, and treasure hidden by smugglers or pirates. In some parts of the world, people have even built homes, storage areas, and places of worship inside caves.

Eco Facts

Caves are full of interesting structures, including stalactites and stalagmites. Stalactites form on the ceilings of caves, and stalagmites form on the cave floor. Both look like giant stone icicles.

Levels of Organization in Cave Ecosystems

Ecosystems can be broken down into levels of organization. These levels range from a single plant or animal to many **species** of plants and animals living together in an area.

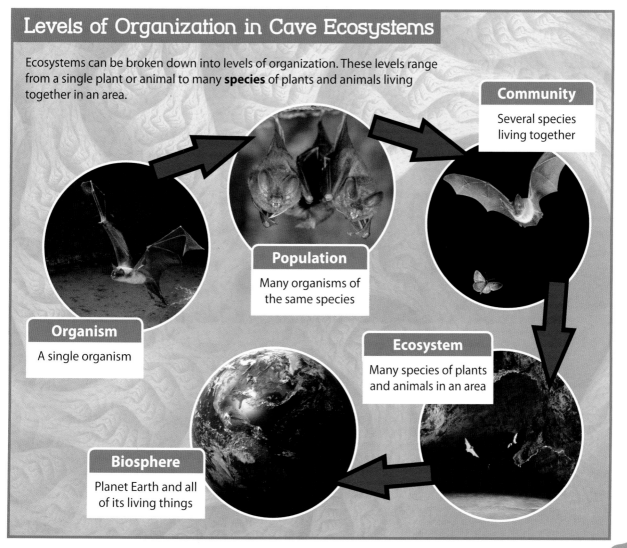

Community
Several species living together

Population
Many organisms of the same species

Organism
A single organism

Ecosystem
Many species of plants and animals in an area

Biosphere
Planet Earth and all of its living things

Where in the World?

Limestone cliffs on the coast of Greece have been carved out by a constant barrage of ocean waves.

Caves lie beneath the ground of every continent of the world. Cave systems extend for great distances and to extreme depths. Some caves even exist beneath towns and cities.

Most caves are located in karst regions. Karst refers to ground that is largely made up of limestone. Limestone is a soft stone that formed millions of years ago from the remains of sea creatures. Scientists estimate that nearly 10 percent of Earth's land surface is made up of karst.

Most of the world's caves formed over many years, as water and wind wore away at the karst and dug out underground tunnels and caverns. Some cave networks are very small, while others are enormous.

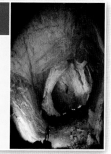

Eco Facts

Scientists believe there are cave systems deeper than 8,300 feet (2,530 m) that have yet to be discovered. That is deeper beneath Earth's surface than any human being has ever traveled.

Mammoth Cave, which is located in Kentucky, has more than 392 miles (631 kilometers) of explored passageways. This is about three times longer than any other cave system in the world. In fact, geologists estimate that there could still be as much as 600 miles (966 km) of unexplored passages in this system.

Sarawak Chamber is the largest known cavern in the world. It is part of Good Luck Cave, which is part of the Mulu cave system in Malaysia. The cavern is 2,297 feet (700 meters) long, 230 feet (70 m) tall and 1,312 feet (400 m) wide. This is big enough to hold more than 7,500 buses.

Some cave systems do not have deep caverns, but are made up of long passageways. In central Asia, the main tunnel of the Boj-Bulok Cave runs more than 4,642 feet (1,415 m) underground, but it is only an average of 20 inches (0.5 m) wide.

Deer Cave, a part of the Mulu cave system in Malaysia, is one of the largest cave passages in the world.

Mapping the Caves

This map shows where some of the world's major cave systems can be found. Find the place where you live on the map. Is it above a cave or cave system? If not, where is the closest cave or cave system to you?

Legend

 Cave

 Ocean

River

Scale at Equator

```
0      1,000    2,000  3,000 miles
|--------|--------|--------|
0   1,000  2,000    3,000 km
```

N

ARCTIC OCEAN

NORTH PACIFIC OCEAN

NORTH AMERICA

Jewel Cave, United States

Carlsbad Caverns, United States

NORTH ATLANTIC OCEAN

Ox Bel Ha Cave System, Mexico

EQUATOR

SOUTH AMERICA

SOUTH PACIFIC OCEAN

Toca da Boa Vista, Brazil

Mammoth Cave

Location: Kentucky, United States
Size: 392 miles (631 km) long
Fact: The longest cave system in the world, Mammoth Cave is about three times longer than the next longest cave system. In fact, if the second and third longest caves in the world were joined together, Mammoth Cave would still be more than 100 miles (161 km) longer.

Krubera Cave

Location: Georgia
Size: 7,188 feet (2,191 m) deep
Fact: Krubera Cave is the deepest known cave in the world. It is the only known cave system to plunge more than 6,562 feet (2,000 m) underground. In 2004, cave explorers named what was then Krubera's deepest chamber, "Game Over." However, passages even deeper than Game Over were discovered in 2007.

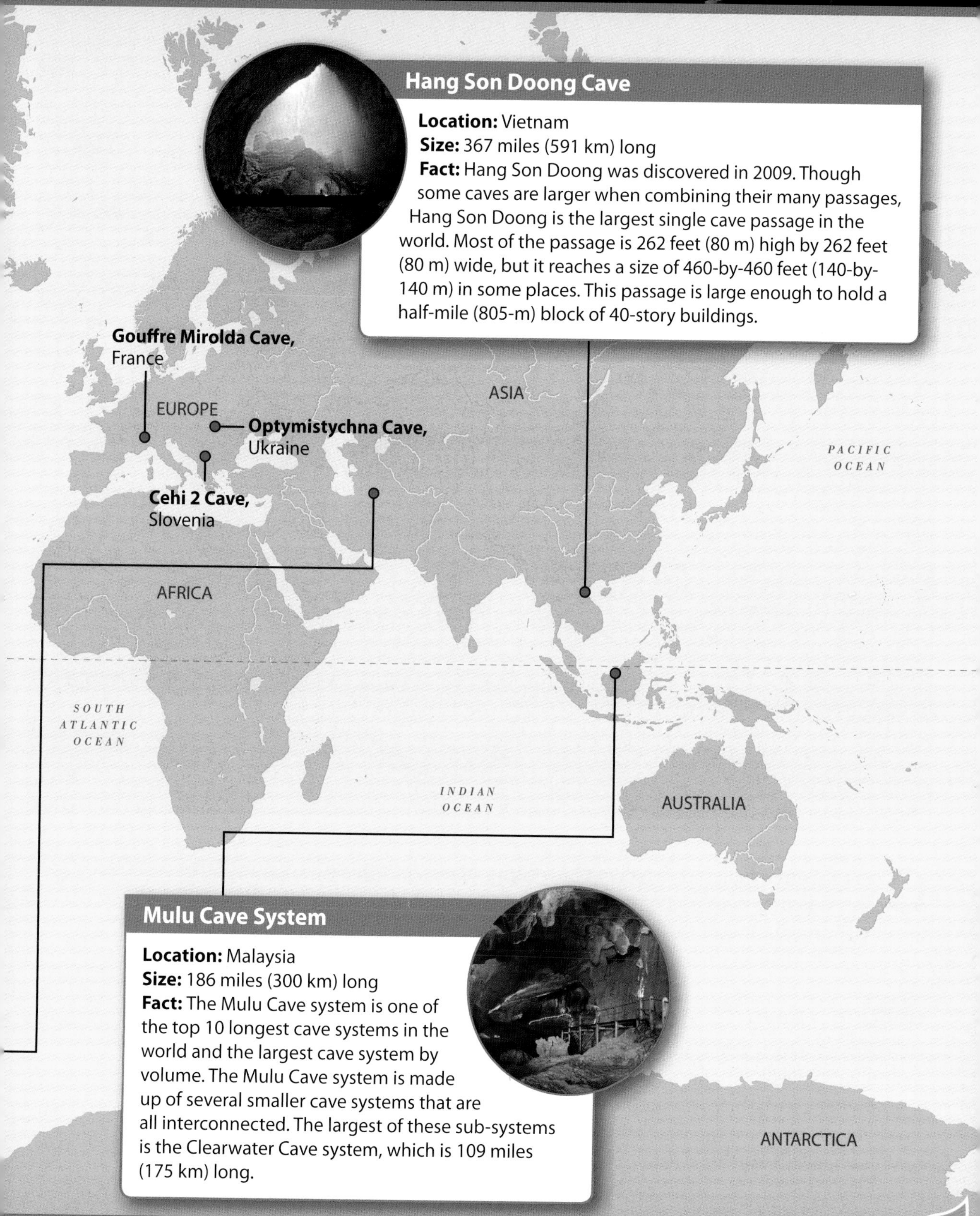

Hang Son Doong Cave

Location: Vietnam
Size: 367 miles (591 km) long
Fact: Hang Son Doong was discovered in 2009. Though some caves are larger when combining their many passages, Hang Son Doong is the largest single cave passage in the world. Most of the passage is 262 feet (80 m) high by 262 feet (80 m) wide, but it reaches a size of 460-by-460 feet (140-by-140 m) in some places. This passage is large enough to hold a half-mile (805-m) block of 40-story buildings.

Gouffre Mirolda Cave,
France

EUROPE

ASIA

Optymistychna Cave,
Ukraine

PACIFIC
OCEAN

Cehi 2 Cave,
Slovenia

AFRICA

SOUTH
ATLANTIC
OCEAN

INDIAN
OCEAN

AUSTRALIA

Mulu Cave System

Location: Malaysia
Size: 186 miles (300 km) long
Fact: The Mulu Cave system is one of the top 10 longest cave systems in the world and the largest cave system by volume. The Mulu Cave system is made up of several smaller cave systems that are all interconnected. The largest of these sub-systems is the Clearwater Cave system, which is 109 miles (175 km) long.

ANTARCTICA

Cave Climate

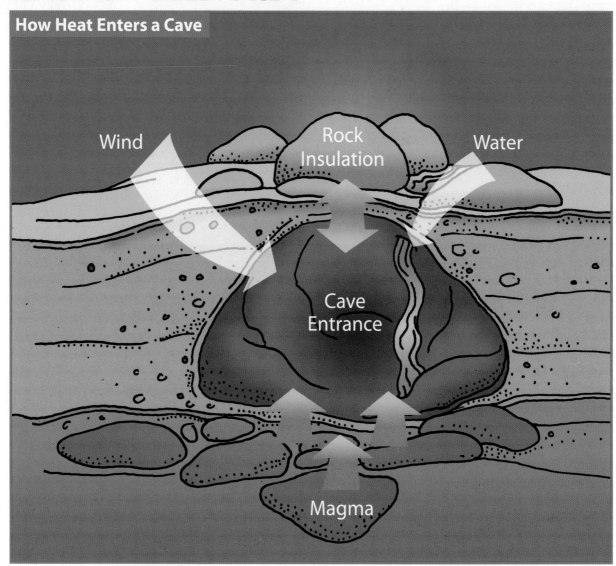

Wind

Rock Insulation

Water

Cave Entrance

Magma

Caves are often believed to be cold and damp places, but this is not always the case. Whether they are hot or cold, dry or wet depends on their location and the environment around them. Sometimes, the inside of a cave can have warmer temperatures than the area outside of the cave.

Heating a Cave

Heat can enter a cave in four ways. Wind can blow heat in through the cave opening. Water flowing into the cave can also bring outside temperatures with it. Rocks lying above the cave can provide **insulation** and help keep the inside warm. Rocks below the cave can also bring warmth as a result of the hot **magma** that bubbles beneath Earth's crust.

Outside Weather

Outside weather can affect more than just the cave's temperature. **Humidity** levels can be affected as well. This occurs when cold air comes into the cave. Cold air is normally dry, and cave air tends to be moist. When the cold air enters the cave, it dries the air inside, making it less humid. As the moisture evaporates, the air becomes cooler, and the temperature inside the cave lowers.

Eco Facts

Their underground location gives caves one of the most unique climates in the world. Rain never falls in caves, but rain aboveground influences the flow of underground streams, rivers, lakes, and even waterfalls.

Precipitation and Air Pressure

External **precipitation** and wind can affect the inside of a cave on a grander scale, depending on where in the world the cave is located. In areas that receive large amounts of rain, such as parts of South America and Asia, caves sometimes flood during the monsoon, or rainy, season. Wind also whistles and blows through some caves, affecting the air pressure inside. When the air pressure outside of a cave increases, more air is forced into the cave, increasing the air pressure inside. When the air pressure outside drops, some of the air inside the cave flows out, reducing the air pressure in the cave as well. A slight breeze develops in the cave as the air rushes in and out. This process helps the air circulate within the cave.

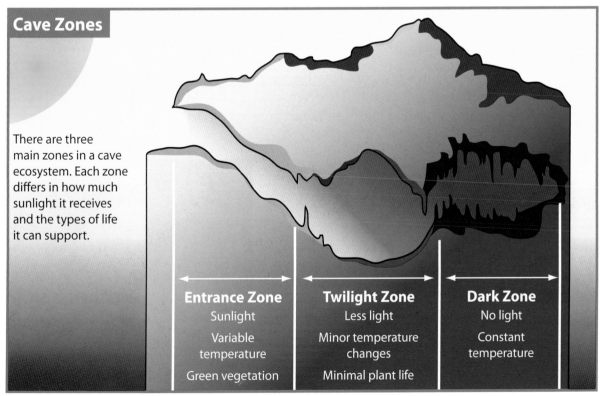

Cave Zones

There are three main zones in a cave ecosystem. Each zone differs in how much sunlight it receives and the types of life it can support.

Entrance Zone	Twilight Zone	Dark Zone
Sunlight	Less light	No light
Variable temperature	Minor temperature changes	Constant temperature
Green vegetation	Minimal plant life	

Types of Caves

Water runoff from storms and melting snow often drains into cave systems.

Caves develop in a variety of ways. They have been one of Earth's landforms for thousands, even millions, of years. However, some caves are more recent in their development. Still others are more temporary in nature, relying on the climate for their longevity.

Sandstone Caves

Millions of years ago, shallow seas covered parts of the planet. Over time, the water dropped, and the sand that had once covered the sea floor was pressed into solid rock called sandstone. Water from rivers and lakes slowly carved out the chambers and tunnels that became sandstone caves.

Water and wind erosion created the graceful curves found in the sandstone of Arizona's Grotto Cave.

Limestone Caves

Long ago, millions of organisms lived in the shallow seas that covered Earth. When these organisms died, their bodies sank to the bottom of the seas and decomposed, or broke down. The weight of the water caused these shells and bones to form hard layers of rock called limestone. Over time, the limestone rose above the ground, where it was carved out further by wind and water. Limestone caves resulted from this process.

Caves are still forming in the limestone of Blue Lake Cave in Brazil.

The rocky coast of California features several sea caves.

Sea Caves

Deep beneath the sea, powerful currents and waves wear rock away to form underwater caves. Waves slowly erode, or wear away, rock from cliff surfaces until pockets form at their bases. As water seeps into these pockets, caves continue to grow. Some sea caves have areas that are above water and other parts that are submerged.

Lava-Tube Caves

When a volcano erupts, magma is released. When magma is aboveground, it is called lava. The lava is so hot, its surface cools before its interior does. The surface hardens as it cools, forming large tunnels or tubes beneath. The molten lava continues to run through these tubes until the eruption stops. The tubes then remain until the next eruption.

The volcanic island of Santa Cruz in the Galapagos Islands is covered with lava-tube caves that can be explored.

Most glacier caves can only be explored when the floor is frozen. During periods of melt, these cave tunnels can be filled with water.

Glacier Caves

Glacier caves are created by the movement of glaciers. As glaciers move across the ground, they melt. Meltwater runs beneath them and hollows out caves inside the glaciers. These caves form and melt very quickly.

Life in a Cave

aves may not seem like the most appealing places to live, but they are home to hundreds of crawling, leaping, and swimming creatures. Organisms that live in cave ecosystems have **adapted** to life in this environment.

Producers

Plants found in the entrance zone of caves act as producers for other organisms in the ecosystem. Producers absorb energy from the Sun and convert it into usable forms of energy such as sugar. Producers make this energy through a process called **photosynthesis.** Producers found in caves include mosses, algae, and low-growing plants that require little sunlight to survive.

Decomposers

Fungi, such as mushrooms and mold, and many types of bacteria live in cave ecosystems. These organisms are called decomposers because they eat dead and decaying organic materials. Decomposers speed up the process of breaking down dead **organic** materials and releasing their **nutrients** into the environment. These nutrients then serve as food for other organisms. In the twilight and dark zones of cave ecosystems, decomposers serve as the main food source for many consumers.

Cave Energy Pyramid

The transfer of energy in an ecosystem begins with producers and moves up the energy pyramid to the tertiary consumers. Organisms at each level of the pyramid receive energy from the organisms in the level below them.

Outside of the pyramid are the decomposers. They break down the dead and decaying organic matter left behind when plants and animals die. For this reason, decomposers receive energy from organisms in all levels of the energy pyramid.

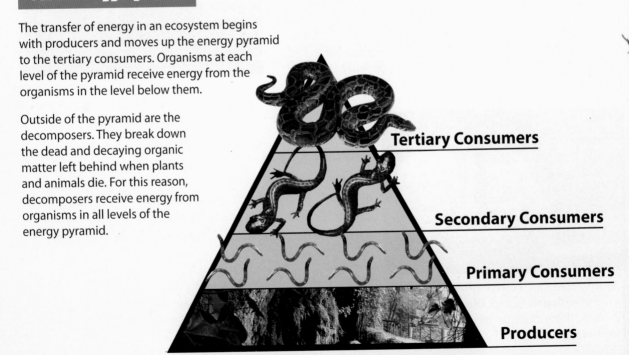

Tertiary Consumers

Secondary Consumers

Primary Consumers

Producers

Caue Food Web

Another way to study the flow of energy through an ecosystem is by examining food chains and food webs. A food chain shows how a producer feeds a primary consumer, which then feeds a secondary consumer, and so on. However, most organisms feed on many different food sources. This practice causes food chains to interconnect, creating a food web.

In this example, the blue line represents one food chain from the moss, roundworm, bat, and spotted python. The red line from the algae, cockroach, bat, and spotted python form another food chain. These food chains connect at the bat, but they also connect in other places. The cockroach feeds from moss as well, and the roundworm also eats algae. This series of connections forms a complex food web.

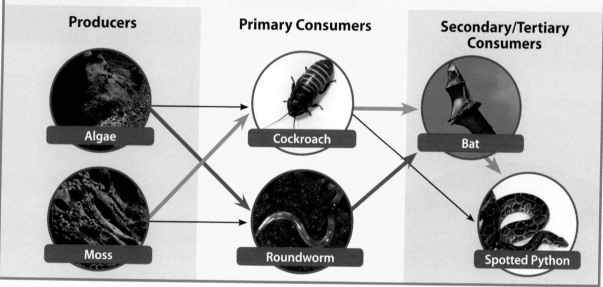

Primary Consumers

The insects and animals that rely on producers as a food source are called primary consumers. When a primary consumer feeds on a producer, the energy made by the producer is transferred to the primary consumer. Primary consumers in cave ecosystems include insects, such as cockroaches, and roundworms.

Secondary and Tertiary Consumers

Secondary consumers feed on both producers and primary consumers. In caves, secondary consumers include insects, such as beetles and spiders, mammals, including bats, and amphibians, such as the cave salamander. Larger carnivores, such as pythons, are called tertiary consumers. Tertiary consumers feed on secondary consumers.

Plants, Fungi, and Lichens

Cave Plants

Despite the lack of sunlight and water, caves have plant life of their own. The type of plants found depends on the cave's surroundings, where it is located, and the climate of the region it is in. Most plant life can be found in the entrance zone of a cave, where sunlight reaches. No plants or trees grow in the dark zone of a cave because plants depend on sunlight to survive. Mosses and ferns are the most common plants found in caves. They grow in the damp entrance zone. Mosses grow well in cave ecosystems because they do not have roots. Instead, they attach themselves to rocks with rootlike structures called rhizoids.

Plant life in caves usually becomes thicker and more diverse as it gets closer to the cave's entrance.

Fungi

Fungi are other organisms found in cave ecosystems. They grow well in caves because the items that they feed on are often present. Dead animals, droppings, and the dead leaves, stems, and twigs carried by underground streams can all be found in caves. Fungi play an important role in cave ecosystems. In twilight and dark zones, fungi act like producers. They decompose organic material, such as **guano**, into food and nutrients. This energy is then passed on to other animals in the cave ecosystem through the food chain.

Fungi thrive in dark, damp caves because they do not need light to grow.

Eco Facts

Crustose lichens form a thick crust on the surface of the object on which they grow. Sometimes, they even embed themselves in the object. Removing them from this spot can be very difficult.

Some mushroom farmers grow their crops in caves because these fungi do well in the dark, damp earth.

Lichens

Lichens grow in most caves. Like mosses, lichens have no roots, so they can grow on rocky surfaces. Lichens come in many colors, including red, yellow, and orange, but most are brown or gray. One type of lichen that grows in caves is crustose lichen. This lichen grows close to the ground, is hard to the touch, and has a scaly appearance. Foliose is another type of lichen that thrives in caves. It grows in leaflike shapes.

Lichens are often found growing on rock.

Mammals and Birds

Mammals

Mammals inhabit the entrance and twilight zones of cave ecosystems. Small mammals, such as mice, rats, voles, and raccoons, move between the shelter of a cave and the world beyond. Large mammals, such as bears, frequently use caves to hibernate during winter. The most common mammal found in the twilight zone is the bat. Hundreds of bat species live in caves around the world, including gray, brown, and pipistrelle bats. In more tropical climates, big cats, such as jaguars, take shelter in caves.

Raccoons sometimes make their home in caves that are near water.

Bats

The most common type of mammal found in cave ecosystems is the bat. Hundreds of species of bats live in caves around the world. Some take shelter and sleep in the caves during the day and leave to hunt at night. Others never leave. Bats can find their way around in dark caves because they use sound to help them detect where they are going. They project high-pitched sounds that bounce back from an object to let them know it is there. Fruit bats are one of the most common types of bats to take shelter in caves, especially in tropical climates. They roost, or hang, in caves during the day and leave at night in search of fruit to eat.

The fringe-lipped bats of South America are known for eating frogs.

Eco Facts

Like bats, oilbirds use sound to help them navigate and find food.

Vultures often live in caves. They prey on the meat of animals that have been killed by other animals, humans, or vehicles.

There are nearly 1,000 bat species in the world. Most bats eat insects, fruit, small animals, or fish, but some eat other bats.

Birds

There may not seem like many places in a cave for birds to swoop and soar, but some species find shelter and build nests in the entrance and twilight zones of caves. Birds such as owls and phoebes make their nests on ledges along cave walls. Two species of birds commonly found in caves are the swiftlet and barn owl. These birds build their nests on the cliff surfaces of the twilight zone of caves throughout North America and Europe. The guacharo, or oilbird, is a type of bird commonly found in the caves of South America and the Caribbean. These rare birds have a wingspan of up to 3 feet (0.91 m). Guacharos are nocturnal, which means they are active at night.

Barn owls leave their caves at night to hunt for food.

Reptiles, Amphibians, Fish, and Invertebrates

Reptiles

Reptiles are cold-blooded animals that are born on land. Being cold-blooded means they rely on the temperature of their surroundings to regulate their body temperature. Reptiles can be found in the entrance and twilight zones of caves and include various snakes and turtles. Snakes, such as copperheads and rattlesnakes, live and hunt in caves. Box turtles, which get their name because of their hinged shell, also find refuge in cave ecosystems. Other reptiles that are not normally found in caves, such as crocodiles, have been discovered in the Ankarana Cave in Africa. Scientists believe that one of the reasons crocodiles adapted to living in caves was to escape being hunted by humans.

In nature, box turtles may live to 100 years of age.

Amphibians

Amphibians are also cold-blooded, but they are born in water. They can be found in all three cave zones. Amphibians enjoy the cool temperatures and damp conditions that caves provide. The most common amphibian found in cave ecosystems is the salamander. The redback salamander is gray in color, with a red or orange stripe running down its back and tail. It is often found near cave entrances. To escape from danger, this salamander coils up and tucks its tail under its head. It then wiggles its tail to distract the predator. If part of the tail is removed by the predator, it will grow back. Texas blind salamanders have colorful red gills around their heads. It looks like they have no eyes. In fact, their eyes are beneath their skin, so they cannot see.

Besides caves, salamanders can also be found under logs or rocks, as well as near streams and other moist areas.

Fish

Though many cave ecosystems only have shallow pools of water, these pools often contain fish and other aquatic life. Caves carved out by the oceans or seas often have tidal pools in their entrance or twilight zones. Waves wash and pull sea creatures into and out of the cave. Some caves also have marine life in their dark zones. One type of fish commonly found in the dark zone is the blind cavefish. Blind cavefish are the most common type of fish found in the caves of North and Central America. Like blind salamanders, some blind cavefish have eyes beneath their skin. Still, many blind cavefish have no eyes at all. They use water vibrations to detect objects and prey in front of them as they swim through the water.

Blind cavefish have adapted to living in the dark. They have no pigment, or color, in their skin because it is never exposed to sunlight.

Invertebrates

Invertebrates are animals that do not have a spinal column, or backbone. This includes insects, **arachnids**, and **crustaceans**. Invertebrates live in all three cave zones. Examples include moths, crickets, spiders, and crayfish. In the Waitomo Glowworm Caves of New Zealand, the dark zones are often illuminated with what looks like a sky full of stars. This light actually comes from glowworms. Glowworms have glands on their abdomen or tail that emit light. They use this light to attract prey. Once they have attracted prey, glowworms catch their prey in a long feeding line. A feeding line is like a spider's web. Glowworms use up to 70 feeding lines to trap insects.

Some glowworm feeding lines are 8 inches (20 cm) long.

Caves in Danger

Scientists work hard to find ways to protect Earth's ecosystems. The greatest threat caves face is development by humans. Caves have a delicate ecosystem that contains unique animals, some of which can be found in no other ecosystem in the world. Caves also contain rare and delicate rock formations, ancient **fossils**, and rock paintings that give scientists clues to the past, as well as valuable information about how Earth grows and changes.

Mining poses a large threat to cave ecosystems. Drilling for natural gas and oil, and digging for minerals, such as gold, copper, and silver, removes the rock that forms caves and may destroy the caves themselves. Industries are constantly looking for new sources of oil and minerals. Their actions have forced many governments to pass laws protecting cave habitats.

The unique plant and animal life that depends on water for survival is also threatened by pollution. Pollution from the increasing number of cities on Earth seeps into the water that eventually flows underground through caves. Amphibians breathe oxygen through their skin. If there are pollutants in the water, the animals also absorb these in their skin. These pollutants may impair the animal's ability to swim, catch food, and reproduce. Reptiles can experience similar problems. When exposed to harmful pollutants, they may produce eggs

Timeline of Human Activity in Caves

Prehistoric people begin painting the walls inside a series of caves in France. These caves are part of what is today called Lascaux Caves, a system of caves containing some of the oldest remaining examples of Stone Age art.

Austrian researcher Adolf Schmidl makes the first accurate maps of caves. Throughout his career, Schmidl maps many caves around the world.

Scientist Anton Posselt officially discovers the Eisriesenwelt Ice Caves in Austria. Before this, the caves were only known to hunters and poachers. The Eisriesenwelt Ice Caves are the largest ice caves in the world.

15,000 BC — **900 AD** — **1821** — **1842** — **1879** — **1903**

The Hohokam Indians form a community near Colossal Cave in what is today southern Arizona. The Hohokam use the cave for shelter and storage. The cave also serves as a shrine.

Stephen Bishop makes the first map of Mammoth Cave. Bishop, who first explored the cave in 1838, draws the map from memory. The map is published in 1844. It illustrates about 10 miles (16 km) of the cave system.

Wind Cave National Park is created in South Dakota. It is the seventh national park created in the United States. It is also the first cave to be protected by law anywhere in the world.

with thinner shells and have fewer young. Plants also rely on water for survival and are equally affected by pollution. Many species of fern and lichen are now protected in caves around the world as endangered species.

Tourism has also had a negative impact on caves. In order to encourage visitors, bridges, elevators, and roadways have been built within many mighty caverns to make them more accessible. These constructions have sometimes weakened cave walls or disrupted the movement of water, air, or animals within them.

Mining can leave sediment in caves that clog cracks, alter water drainage patterns, and change the cave's humidity. It can also disrupt airflow in the cave.

René Neuville discovers what may be the oldest known human burial site in a cave in Israel.

In Mexico, brothers Juan and Pedro Sanchez discover the Cave of Crystals while drilling a new tunnel in a mine. The cave contains the largest naturally formed crystals found anywhere on Earth. Some of these crystals are up to 36 feet (11 m) long.

A team of three scientists discover the first Stone Age cave art to be found in Great Britain. It is found at Church Cave.

1933   **1940**   **1947**   **2000**   **2003**   **2007**

Four teenage boys from the Vézère Valley in France discover the Lascaux cave complex. The discovery leads to new information about prehistoric humans and their art.

Hundreds of clay jars containing text from the Old Testament of the Bible are found in a network of caves near the Dead Sea, between Israel and Jordan. These texts are now referred to as the Dead Sea Scrolls. The last of these scrolls is discovered in 1956.

Cave divers discover a new passage that establishes Ox Bel Ha as the world's longest underwater cave. Located in the Yucatan Peninsula in Mexico, the underwater cave stretches more than 112 miles (180 km).

Science in Caves

Scientists often rely on climbing and rappelling equipment to explore caves.

Studying caves helps scientists understand how Earth has grown and changed over time. By analyzing the development of caves and the life forms found inside, scientists can gain a better understanding of this unique ecosystem.

Studying Caves

The study of caves is called speleology. Speleology is a branch of geology. This is the study of Earth's formations and composition, and the processes that shape it. Speleology combines geology with the study of other branches of science. One branch is mineralogy, or the study of gems and minerals. Another is hydrology, the study of how water shapes the land. Speleology also combines aspects of biology, the study of living organisms.

Exploring Caves

Speleologists must be good at caving, or exploring a cave. Cavers are skilled at moving through a cave's narrow passages, giant caverns, and sometimes dangerous waterways. Cavers must also be able to climb up and down steep surfaces. They use the same equipment as rock climbers, including strong nylon rope, an **ascender**, and a rappel rack, which controls how fast a person moves down a cliff's side. When exploring dark zones, cavers wear a hard hat that shines a bright light into the area.

Eco Facts

Early explorers who ventured into caves used crude methods to track where they had gone. To make sure they did not get lost, some explorers ran string behind them so they could find their way back out.

Speleologists sometimes spend months at a time beneath the ground studying caves.

Tools

Once inside the cave, speleologists begin their studies using specialized tools. These may include measuring tapes and clinometers, which scientists use to measure angles in caves they are surveying. **Chocks** and **pitons** also help speleologists maneuver through the underground world. One way speleologists study caves and cave networks is through dye gauging. Dye gauging involves releasing dye into a river in a cave to monitor where the water flows. Dye gauging helps determine the size and complexity of a cave system. Advanced methods of dye gauging use leucophor. This clear liquid can be detected under phosphorescent lights so that speleologists can track a river's direction even in the darkest parts of a cave.

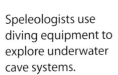
Speleologists use diving equipment to explore underwater cave systems.

Working in Caves

Many caves contain passages that are covered in water. Cave explorers must often pass through these passages, called sumps, in order to reach deeper parts of the cave.

The people who study caves and the plants and animals that live in them have an excellent knowledge of science, history, and math. A good education is needed to study the geology of a cave, the culture and customs of the people who depended on caves, and the wildlife that lives in caves. People who work in caves often study sciences such as geology, biology, anthropology, and speleology.

Speleologist

Duties

Collects and records data from cave environments

Education

Bachelor of science degree

Interests

Earth sciences, cave ecosystems and wildlife, biology, geology

Speleologists study the plants, animals, and geology of caves. Much of their time is spent working underground, sometimes in laboratories set up in the caves. Scientific speleologists can specialize in many areas, including studying the effects of climate change on cave ecosystems.

Other Cave Jobs

Cave Surveyor

Explores caves to record data such as the height, length, and width of the cave, as well as maps the location of cave pathways

Cave Conservationist

Lobbies for the protection of cave ecosystems from human development

Speleobiologist

Studies the plants, animals, and other forms of life found in cave ecosystems

Bill Stone

Bill Stone (1953–) is an American engineer and cave explorer. Stone earned his doctoral degree in structural engineering from the University of Texas in 1980. By that time, he had already been actively exploring caves for almost 10 years.

After graduating, Stone completed a series of challenging cave expeditions around the globe. He quickly earned a reputation as one of the world's most accomplished cave explorers. In more than 40 years of cave exploring, Stone has participated in 44 international cave expeditions.

Exploring caves has given Stone an opportunity to put his engineering skills to good use. In 1980, Stone created a company called Stone Aerospace. Through his company, Stone has created many inventions that help people explore deeper into caves. His most successful invention is a device that cleans carbon dioxide from the air humans breathe out, allowing them to re-breathe the same air.

Stone is currently working with NASA to explore areas that humans cannot. Stone and NASA developed a robot to explore and map areas under the ice in Antarctica in 2009. However, this was just a test run for the real mission. Stone and NASA plan to use the robot to explore Europa, an icy moon orbiting Jupiter, about 485 million miles (780 million km) from Earth.

Cave formations such as stalactites and stalagmites grow over thousands, sometimes millions, of years. In this activity, you can watch them build and grow in your own home or classroom.

Materials

3 saucers

6 jars or cups of the same size

epsom salts

warm water

3 pieces of yarn or string

baking soda (Sodium Bicarbonate)

washing soda (Sodium Carbonate)

1. Place one saucer between two of the jars or cups.

2. Dissolve as much Epsom salt as you can in warm water in each of the containers.

3. Soak a piece of string in the solution. Then, put one end in one container and the other in the second container, with the middle hanging over the saucer. Make sure the string sags in the middle until it is lower than the water level in the two containers.

4. Repeat this process with the other saucers and jars using baking soda and washing soda and the other two pieces of string.

5. Check your experiment each day. What sorts of formations grow on each of the strings? Are there differences between them? Which formations look like the stalactites and stalagmites you might see in a cave?

Create a Food Web

U se this book, and research on the Internet, to create a food web of cave ecosystem plants and animals. Start by finding at least three organisms of each type—producers, primary consumers, secondary consumers, and tertiary consumers. Then, begin linking these organisms together into food chains. Draw the arrows of each food chain in a different color. Use a **red** pen or crayon for one food chain and **green** and **blue** for the others. You should find that many of these food chains connect, creating a food web. Add the rest of the arrows to complete the food web using a pencil or **black** pen.

Once your food web is complete, use it to answer the following questions.

1 How would removing one organism from your food web affect the other organisms in the web?

2 What would happen to the rest of the food web if the producers were taken away?

3 How would decomposers fit into the food web?

Sample Food Web

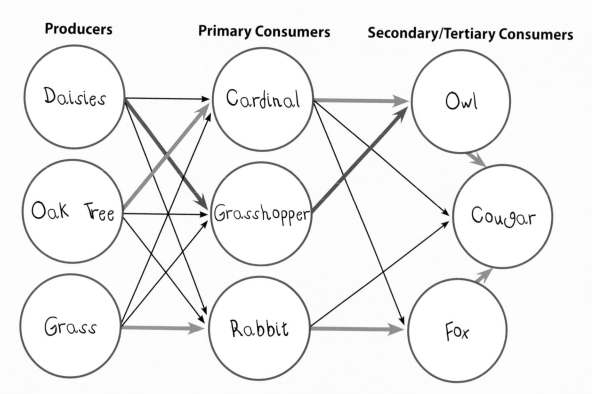

Eco Challenge

1. What are the three zones in a cave?

2. Which is the largest known cavern in the world?

3. What is speleology?

4. What is the difference between a stalactite and a stalagmite?

5. Where can glacier caves be found?

6. How many feeding lines might a glowworm make to catch its prey?

7. What are some of the dangers that threaten caves?

8. What is another name for the oilbird?

9. What do mosses use to attach themselves to rocks?

10. What is the name for a cave passage that is covered in water?

Answers

1. The entrance zone, the twilight zone, and the dark zone
2. The Sarawak Chamber in Malaysia
3. A branch of geology that focuses on the study of caves
4. Stalactites form on the ceilings of caves, and stalagmites form on cave floors.
5. Inside glaciers or icebergs
6. Up to 70
7. Mining, pollution, and tourism
8. The guacharo
9. Rhizoids
10. A sump

Glossary

adapted: changed to fit an environment

arachnids: a group of animals, including spiders, that are related to insects

ascender: equipment that prevents slipping down a rope

caverns: large caves that are mostly underground

chocks: climbing equipment that anchors the climber to the rock

crustaceans: animals with segmented bodies, jointed limbs, and an outer shell

ecosystem: a community of living things sharing an environment

fossils: remains that are preserved in rock

glaciers: large, slow-moving bodies of ice

guano: dung from a bat or sea bird

hibernation: the act of passing the winter in a resting state

humidity: moisture in the air

insulation: material that is used to slow or stop the flow of electricity, heat, or sound

magma: melted rock below Earth's surface

nutrients: substances that feed plants or animals

organic: materials that come from living things

organisms: living things

photosynthesis: the process in which a green plant uses sunlight to change water and carbon dioxide into food for itself

pitons: metal spikes hammered into a rock face to anchor a climber

precipitation: rain, snow, or hail

species: a group of similar plants and animals that can mate together

Index

Log on to www.av2books.com

AV² by Weigl brings you media enhanced books that support active learning. Go to www.av2books.com, and enter the special code found on page 2 of this book. You will gain access to enriched and enhanced content that supplements and complements this book. Content includes video, audio, web links, quizzes, a slide show, and activities.

Audio
Listen to sections of the book read aloud.

Video
Watch informative video clips.

Embedded Weblinks
Gain additional information for research.

Try This!
Complete activities and hands-on experiments.

WHAT'S ONLINE?

Try This!	Embedded Weblinks	Video	EXTRA FEATURES
Map cave systems around the world.	Learn more about caves.	Watch a video about caves.	**Audio** Listen to sections of the book read aloud.
Find out more about animals that live in caves.	Find out more about cave climates.	Watch a video about an animal that lives in a cave.	
Test your knowledge of human activity in caves.	Learn how to identify different plants in caves.		**Key Words** Study vocabulary, and complete a matching word activity.
Write a descriptive paragraph about a day in the life of scientists working in caves.	Read about current research in caves.		**Slide Show** View images and captions, and prepare a presentation
	Learn more about food chains.		**Quizzes** Test your knowledge.

AV² was built to bridge the gap between print and digital. We encourage you to tell us what you like and what you want to see in the future.

Sign up to be an AV² Ambassador at www.av2books.com/ambassador.